An Orange All Round

Lizzie Swanson

Illustrated by
Alexa Rutherford

Andy was leaning on the gate,
swinging open and shut,
open and shut, open and shut.
He had been counting the number of
swings he made.
He'd got to fifty-four.
But now he was bored and had lost
count.

It's a good day for doing something,
Andy thought to himself.
But what could he do?
There was no one else around and
it wasn't much fun going to
the playground alone.

He turned to look towards the
playground, just in time
to see his mum come round the corner.

She was coming back from the shops.
He could see a loaf of bread poking
out of her shopping bag.
Perhaps there was something for him
hidden underneath!
"Have you bought me something, Mum?"
Andy asked.
"Did you get me some sweets?"

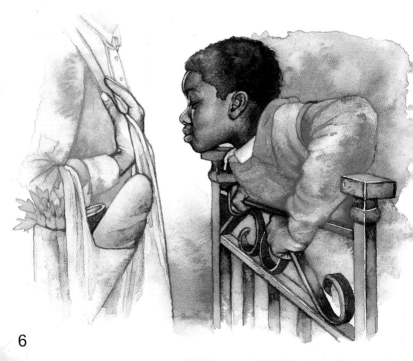

Andy jumped off the gate and opened
it wide so that Mum could get through.
"No, Andy. No sweets today,"
said Mum, and she disappeared into
the house.

Andy was disappointed.
He turned away and
kicked the gate shut with his foot.

But Mum soon came out again.
"No sweets," she said,
"but here's an orange."
She handed Andy an orange that was
so big, he had to use both his hands
to take it. He began to cheer up.

He struggled back onto the gate and
started to peel the orange.
The first bit was the hardest.
He finally used his teeth
to give it a start.

The orange was a fat one,
and looked juicy.
In fact, it **was** juicy.
When Andy pushed too hard with
his fingers, the juice squirted out!

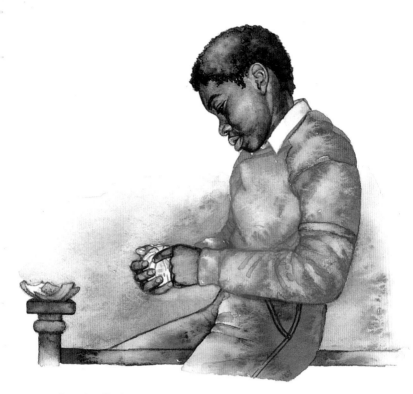

Andy finished peeling the orange and
made a neat pile of the rind on top of
the gatepost.

Then he counted the orange segments
and smiled.

He had twelve pieces of juicy orange
all to himself!

He was just about to
pop the first one into his mouth,
when his sister Ruth came
out of the house.

"Mum says that I can have
half of that orange," said Ruth.
Andy closed his mouth.
This was **his** orange.
Why did he have to
share it with his sister?
But he knew better than to argue.

Slowly and carefully, he divided
the orange into two halves –
six segments for Ruth and
six segments for himself.

Just as Andy was about to
give one half to Ruth,
Dina came up to the gate.
"Ooh, an orange! Can I have some?"
she asked.

Andy looked at his big, juicy orange
and frowned.
It was a big orange, that was for sure.
But it was a big **whole** orange.
It was not so big when it had to be
shared among three people!

Andy had just worked out that
there would be four segments each.
He started to give Dina her share.
"Me, too," came a voice from behind
the fence.

Tom, who lived next door, always appeared whenever food was being handed out.

Andy sighed. Twelve segments. Four people.

"O.K.", he said. "We can have exactly three segments each."

By this time, Penny had joined
the group around Andy's gate.
"You must give Penny some, too,"
said Ruth.
Penny was her best friend.

Andy jumped off the gate and
began to think again.
Twelve segments. Five people.
This was getting difficult.
Then he had an idea.

He would eat two segments quickly,
when no one was looking.
Then he would have ten segments left.
He could share ten segments among
five people by giving each person
two segments.

While he was working this out,
Andy had been walking down the road.
Behind him was Dina who
was talking to Penny, and
Ruth who was boxing with Tom.
At the end of the high wall,
Andy ran round the corner.

Bump!

Andy had run straight into Danny, who fell over.

"Sorry, Danny," said Andy as he helped his friend off the ground.

"Come with us. We're going to share an orange."

So Andy and Danny and Ruth and
Penny and Dina and Tom
all crossed the road to the playground.

Andy sat on a swing and
counted the friends.
One, two, three, four, five, six ... Seven.

Seven?
Lin had joined the group
in the playground.

When there were only six, they
could have had two segments each.
Now Andy stared at his
twelve orange segments.
How could he share them among
seven?

"Hey, you lot! What are you doing?"
Tom's big brother Bert and his mates
had come into the playground.
One, two, three, four, five of them.
Andy counted.
That made twelve people altogether.
Oh dear! He would now get only one
segment from his big, juicy orange!

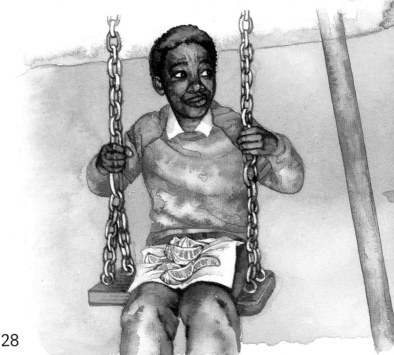

"Who wants some popcorn?"
Bert shouted as he held up a large bag.
And all of Andy's friends rushed over to
Bert and his mates.

Andy stayed on the swing.
One by one he ate each of
the twelve orange segments.
He thought it was the biggest,
the best, and the juiciest orange
he had ever eaten.
What a great day! Lots of friends to
have fun with in the playground and
a whole orange all to himself!